LEO LAMB DISCOVERS
THE PERFECT FRIEND

WRITTEN BY
REBECCA STRAWSON

Copyright © 2024 by Rebecca Strawson

All rights reserved.
All rights reserved. No part of this book may be reproduced or used in any manner without written permission of the copyright owner except for the use of quotations in a book review.

First paperback edition 2024

Written by Rebecca Strawson
Illustrated by Doodle Press

978-1-80541-597-8 (paperback)
978-1-80541-598-5 (hardback)
978-1-80541-596-1 (ebook)

In appreciation of Enid

love Rebecca

It is the morning and Leo Lamb is excited to go to a party with his friends, Zion the Lion and Odette the Owl. Leo Lamb is so excited to sing Happy Birthday and to give a special present to his friend Daniel the Dove.

"Mama can we get a present for Daniel? I don't know what to get him though?" questions Leo Lamb.

"Of course! Let's go to the shops today to get him something special. Quick, let's go!" says Mama Lamb.

"Yay!" shrieks Leo Lamb.

It's a long way to the shops, and on the way Leo Lamb starts feeling bored and tired.

"Are we almost there yet?" pleads Leo Lamb.

"Almost." says Mama Lamb.

(yawn from Leo)

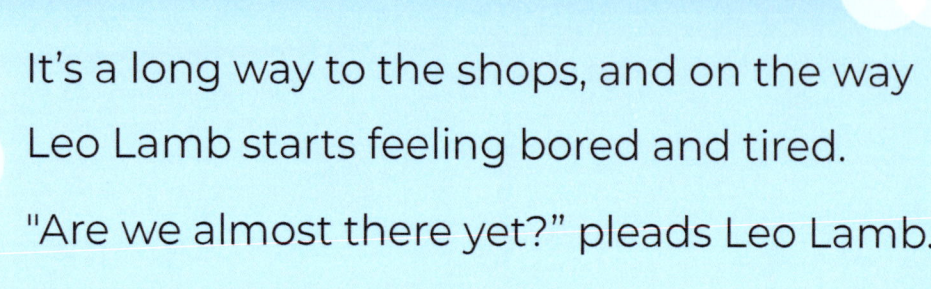

YAAAAWN!

When they arrive at the shops, Leo Lamb isn't very happy so he doesn't want to get Daniel the Dove a present anymore because he is so tired.

Leo Lamb cries and decides to throw away the gifts that Mama Lamb picks out for Daniel the Dove.

"No Mama! I don't want to get Daniel anything. I want to get something special for me." says Leo Lamb.

"I understand. However, let me help you choose something special for Daniel. My friend says that good will come to those who are generous, and that those who give generously will gain more." shares Mama Lamb in wisdom.

Leo Lamb listens to this carefully and decides to find a special present for his friend Daniel the Dove.

"Thank you Mama. Can I meet your friend one day? He sounds perfect!" says Leo Lamb joyfully. *(giggling)*

"Of course you can! He is your friend too. Yes He definitely is perfect!" chuckles Mama Lamb lovingly.

"What a lovely present!" says the shop keeper.

"Thank you!" smiles Leo Lamb "I've bought it with my own pocket money. My friend says we should give generously."

"That is great advice. I should start doing that as well. Your friend really does sound perfect!" smiles the shop keeper.

Mama Lamb and Leo Lamb buy the gift for Daniel the Dove and go home to wrap it up.

When they get home, they wrap the present up and write a nice card for Daniel the Dove to open at the party. Leo Lamb also puts it into a bag to keep it a surprise for Daniel the Dove.

Ding Dong, Ding Dong, Ding Dong.

"It's the bell!" shrieks Leo Lamb excitedly. "I wonder who it could be!" They open the door and find Zion the Lion and Odette the Owl on their doorstep. What a lovely surprise! They have come to meet Leo Lamb at his house so that they can all walk to the party together.

"Are you ready to go to a party?" whispers Mama Lamb. "YES, YES, YES!" shouts Leo Lamb, Zion the Lion and Odette the Owl.

Just as they were about to leave the house, Zion the Lion pushes in front of Leo Lamb and Odette the Owl. Leo Lamb starts crying and walks off feeling upset. He sits on a step and doesn't want to talk until Odette the Owl says

"It's ok. Just like my friend says, forgive those who have hurt us."

Leo Lamb listens quietly and eventually says "Wow your friend sounds like my Mama's friend. He sounds perfect!"

"Sorry Leo and Odette. I shouldn't have pushed in front of you." says Zion the Lion.

"It's ok. We forgive you Zion!" reply Leo Lamb and Odette the Owl in unison.

"Let's go." says Mama Lamb.

They are now at the party and Daniel the Dove has invited all of his friends. They play musical statues and pass the parcel and now it is time to open the presents! Everyone is so excited.

"Which one should I open first?" asks Daniel the Dove.

"Mine!" says Leo Lamb excitedly, leaping off the ground.

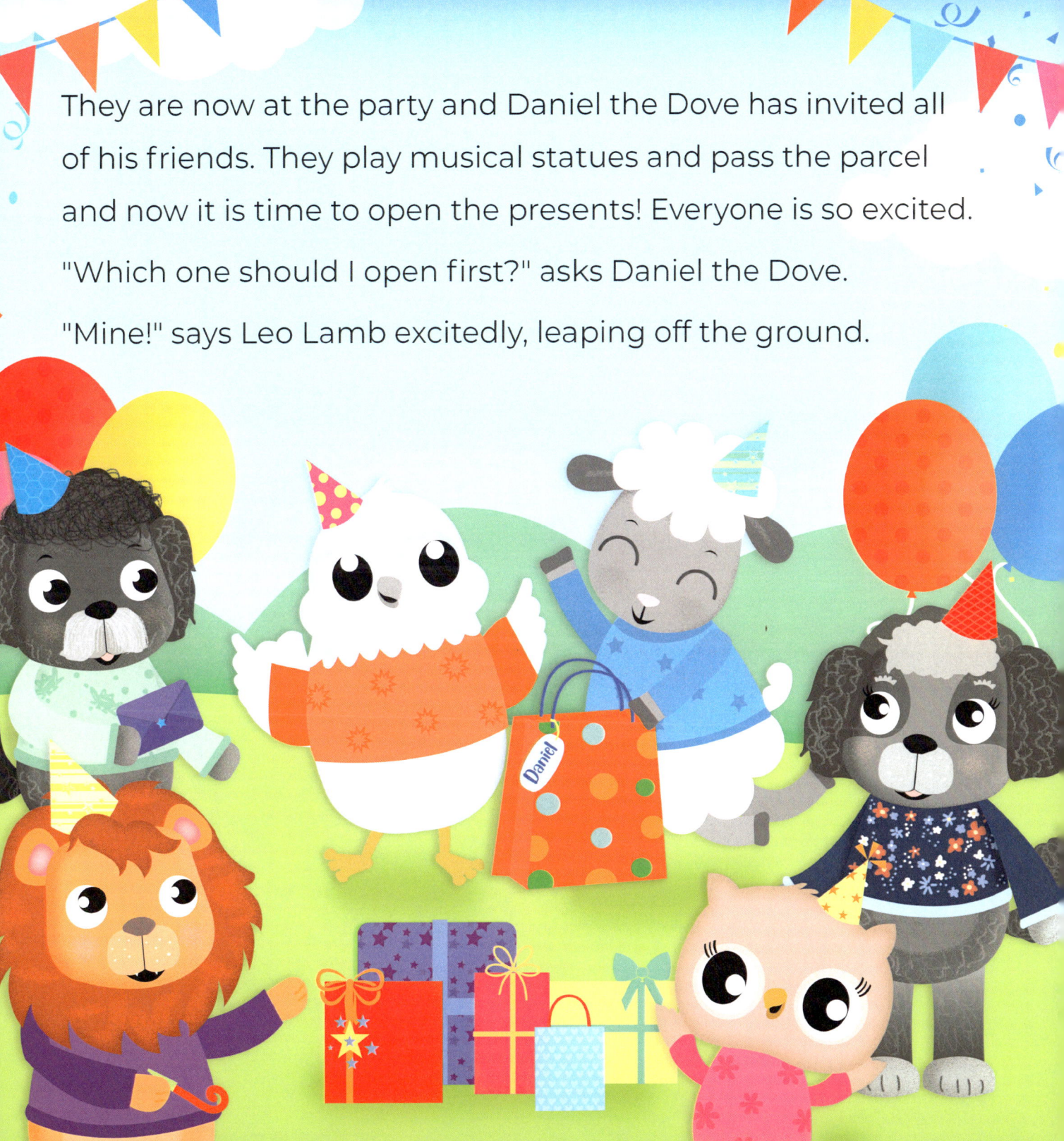

Daniel the Dove starts opening his present and discovers a rainbow hat in the bag!

"Wow, I love it!" thanks Daniel the Dove.

But just as he was about to put the hat on... it blew away in the wind!

Oh no!

Daniel the Dove begins to cry and Leo Lamb is not happy either, and hits and kicks his Mama when she tries to comfort him.

Mama Lamb calmly says "We can sort it out. I don't want you to hit or kick me because it hurts me. I forgive you though. My friend says to learn to be loving, kind and gentle. It is called the fruits of the spirit and those are just a few!"

Leo Lamb listens carefully and says "Wow. I want to be a person like that!

Your friend sounds perfect! Sorry Mama for hitting and kicking you."

When it was time for Leo Lamb to go home, they agree to find an even more special gift for Daniel the Dove in the morning.

It is dark outside and time for bed, so Mama Lamb starts to get Leo Lamb ready for bed.

"What is your friends name? He sounds so perfect and I want Him to be my friend too!" exclaims Leo Lamb.

"His name is Jesus. You are so right. He is perfect and He loves you so much!" says Mama Lamb happily.

"I love Jesus too, but where can I find the wise words that He tells you Mama?" asks Leo Lamb.

"It is called the bible and it has 66 books in it. How awesome is that? Jesus is definitely your perfect friend and He is always with you. Jesus is the light in the darkness!" shares Mama Lamb proudly.

"Wow! He truly is my new perfect friend and my light. I'm going to invite him on all the adventures that we go on Mama! I know. Let's get Daniel a bible for his birthday. That is the most special gift ever." whispers Leo Lamb as he falls asleep.

"You're absolutely right. What a great idea. Night night, Leo" says Mama Lamb lovingly.

www.ingramcontent.com/pod-product-compliance
Lightning Source LLC
Chambersburg PA
CBRC091724070526
44585CB00008B/165